WITHDRAWN

MY WILD LIFE

Adventures of a Wildlife Photographer

By Suzi Eszterhas

Owlkids Books

Contents

My childhood dreams

I knew I wanted to be a wildlife photographer since I was a young girl. I told my parents that I wanted to live in a tent in Africa. They encouraged me and taught me never to give up on my dreams.

When I was six, I got my first camera. I didn't travel to exotic places when I was a kid, so my early adventures happened close to home. In this photo, I look like I'm on safari, but I'm actually at a local zoo.

I loved taking pictures of my cats in my backyard. I pretended they were lions and tigers in the wild. I also loved to just sit under a tree and feel close to nature. I spent hours watching squirrels and birds. I wrote down everything they did in my field book. I felt like Jane Goodall studying chimpanzees in the wild.

I didn't know it at the time, but all those hours I spent sitting quietly in nature were great training for being a wildlife photographer. Some days, it's all I do for hours at a time.

I've been a professional wildlife photographer for over twenty years. I love my work, but it hasn't all been easy. I've faced a lot of challenges: raising money to go on distant photo shoots, staying safe while traveling alone in wild and remote areas, and showing people that women can be wildlife photographers, too. And that list doesn't include the animals. They can be difficult to reach, tricky to photograph, and downright dangerous when they feel threatened.

One important thing I've learned is to keep an open mind and stay ready for any adventure—and there have been lots! Some of my wildest include hugging a baby whale, swimming with sloths, fending off a curious grizzly bear with a baseball cap, and raising an orphaned wildcat kitten so he could return to the wild.

Today, I travel the world to take pictures of wild animals.
I feel so lucky to have a job that I love!

World travels

A big part of my job is traveling to the wild places where animals live. I spend nearly half of each year away from home on photo shoots. I've visited all seven continents and seen hundreds of animal species. There are still many more that I want to see.

I usually spend weeks or even months at a time on location, photographing animals in their natural habitats. While I am there, I must adapt to the conditions—and they can be extreme!

Polar Bear

Orcas

Toucan

When I photographed polar bears in the Arctic, I stayed outside on the frozen tundra all day long. Some days, the temperature dropped to forty degrees below zero! To stay warm, I bundled up in layers of clothing— sometimes more than seven. I had to learn special techniques to keep my cameras from freezing, too.

Penguins

Panda Bear

Chimpanzees

I've been everywhere from freezing polar regions to scorching deserts, and each habitat has unique challenges. Steamy, hot jungles have been some of the most trying. The weather can make you sweaty and uncomfortable, and the critters can be even worse. Some of them like to get a little too close for my comfort. While I was photographing chimps in Uganda, I woke up to find ticks and beetles in my nose! Bugs even laid eggs in the soles of my feet. Gross! I was also chased by a green mamba—one of the world's deadliest snakes—and swarmed by bees.

Prepping for shoots

The goal of every photo shoot is to get great shots of animals doing interesting things. It takes a bit of luck to get these photos. More importantly, it takes a lot of preparation.

I always read as much as I can about my subjects before I go on a shoot. I talk to animal experts, too. The information I gather helps me to predict what an animal might do and when. It helps improve my chances of capturing the action.

Knowing how animals behave also helps keep me safe. Wild animals can be dangerous, but usually they attack only if they feel threatened. Learning what my subjects find threatening helps me avoid upsetting them and putting myself in danger. It also helps me recognize their warnings.

When a silverback gorilla charged at me in Rwanda, I knew not to panic. Seeing a huge, angry gorilla rush at you is scary, but this behavior is almost always a warning. The silverback was just letting me know that he was in charge. I stood back to show that I was not a threat, and he didn't attack.

This massive silverback gorilla is beating his chest, getting ready to charge at me.

Out in the wild, I often have only a few seconds to capture a perfect shot. Before I leave on a shoot, I always practice using new equipment and techniques. Sometimes I have a dream shot in my mind. Practice shoots help me figure out how I can create that image. That way, when I am in the field with my animal, I know exactly what to do. I can do it very quickly before I miss the moment.

When I planned to photograph swimming sloths in Panama, I had never taken pictures under water before. So I practiced in a swimming pool, using a teddy bear as my model. My practice paid off, and I captured this swimming sloth perfectly. This photo appeared on the cover of my book Sloths: Life in the Slow Lane.

Animals roam freely through a bush camp. Elephants were some of my most exciting visitors. They can be dangerous if you walk near them, so I often hid inside my tent until they left.

Living in the field

One of the most exciting parts of my job is that I get to live in interesting places to be close to my wild subjects. I have lived aboard boats, slept on villagers' floors, and lived in mountain cabins and bush camps. This can be a challenge, but it is always an adventure!

Sometimes I am lucky, and there is an ecolodge near the wildlife I want to photograph. Ecolodges are like hotels in wilderness areas or national parks. They are very comfortable—sometimes even fancy.

In remote places, I usually camp. I have lived in a tent for weeks, months, even years at a time. Often there is no electricity, so I charge my cameras and computer with a car battery or solar panels. Sometimes there are no bathrooms, either. I lived in a tent in Kenya—without a toilet—for three years. I'd only planned to spend a couple of months there. But I loved living so close to nature that I stayed.

Sleeping in a tent lets me live near animals without disturbing them. There are usually no fences around the camp, so animals come and go anytime. Through the canvas walls of my tent, I've heard lions roaring and hippos blowing bubbles in a river. I've watched zebras grazing next to me and an elephant munching on the trees above me. Once, a leopard rested in the moonlight outside my tent door!

This was my shower while I lived in Kenya. I heated water over the fire, so I had warm—but short—showers. I've lived in other places where a shower wasn't even an option. I once went a whole month without showering!

Solar panels helped me keep my cameras charged and ready for action in a remote jungle in Guyana.

This tent in Kenya was my home for three years. The serval cat was an orphan that I raised and returned to the wild. His name is Moto.

Game drives

GUIDE SEAT

MARUTI

Shubh

While living in the field, I often go on game drives to find animals to photograph. Game drives are treks into the wilderness in 4x4 vehicles. They are pretty common in Africa and India, so animals there are used to seeing people in 4x4s. On one game drive, a tiger felt so comfortable that it walked right under my jeep!

Some of my first game drives were in the Masai Mara, a huge game reserve in Kenya. I spent many months with cheetahs, following them in my jeep all day, every day. The cheetahs got so used to seeing me that, to them, I became part of the landscape, like a tree or a boulder.

Some of the cheetah cubs I worked with became so used to my presence that they played on my jeep's tires or rested in its shade.

Rhinos are enormous, powerful animals. They are known to charge when they feel threatened. A game drive is the safest way to see rhinos in the wild.

I'm on my own for most game drives. I usually head out before sunrise, when it is still dark, and I stay out until the sun sets. I often spend hours driving through the bush, searching for animals. Sometimes there are no roads, so I must drive over rocks, through mud, and across shallow rivers to find my subjects.

When I lived in the Masai Mara, I drove a small jeep all over the savannah. There is no roadside service in the bush, so when I got a flat tire, I had to fix it myself. And when I drove off-road, I learned how to avoid getting stuck in mud or in big holes made by aardvarks. I did get stuck a few times, though, and once I had to wait sixteen hours for someone to find me.

Animals are unpredictable. Some days, I don't see my subjects at all. Other days, the action never stops. One day in India, I watched these tiger cubs sleep in the brush all day before they suddenly woke up and started playing at a nearby water hole.

Going undercover

Some animals are easy subjects. I can simply walk or drive alongside them and take their picture without scaring them. For other animals, the sight of me on foot or in a car can be very scary, so I must be careful how I approach them. Often, I can only photograph these animals by hiding.

Sometimes, I dress in camouflage from head to toe so that I blend in with the surroundings, and animals can't see me. Other times, I spend hours or days inside a small structure called a *blind*. It can be a camouflage tent or a mud hut that looks exactly like the animal's habitat.

I stay completely still and quiet inside a blind so that the animals don't hear me. I spend hours at a time huddled up, not moving. If I have an itch, I can't even scratch it!

I clearly mark my pee bottle. I don't want to mix it up with my water bottle!

Animals can be frightened by the smell of humans, too. So when I need to use the bathroom, I don't go outside. I use a pee bottle inside the blind instead. I make sure it is clearly labeled!

The most exciting thing about being in a blind is that you never know what is going to happen or who is going to show up. Once, I was waiting in a blind near a water hole, hoping to see a beautiful bird. Instead, a bobcat came for a drink!

Blinds are the best way to get close to shy, small birds, such as this honeycreeper I photographed in Costa Rica.

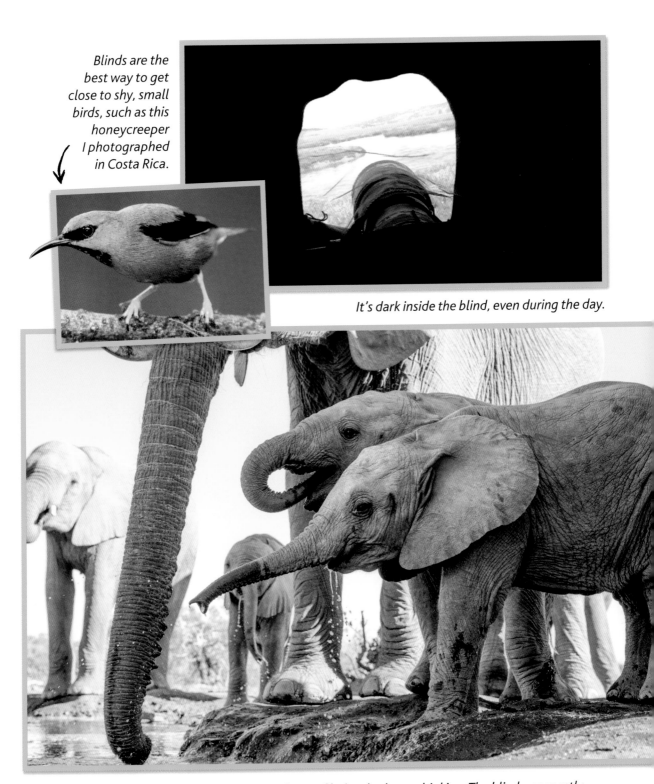

It's dark inside the blind, even during the day.

I sat in a blind at a water hole to get this photo of baby elephants drinking. The blind was mostly underground, so my camera peeked out of a hole at water level. This allowed me to be at the elephants' level without disturbing their afternoon drink.

15

Highs and lows

Whenever possible, I like to be at eye level with the wildlife I am photographing. This helps me create a powerful image with eye contact, so it seems as though the animal is looking right at you. It also helps me see better into the animal's world.

I've gone to dizzying heights to reach animals that live in trees. One time, I climbed jungle trees to get closer to sloths. Another time, I got a lift in a bucket truck to get eye-level photos of birds nesting in treetops.

For eye contact with animals such as reptiles and amphibians, I must get down low on the ground. I've spent hours lying on my belly in the dirt or mud. This is usually at night when these species are most active. That means I am up all night and asleep all day.

People may not think of insects as wildlife, but they are! Bees and other insects are a challenge because of their small size. Just imagine how tiny a bee's eyes are! Making eye contact with bees means getting on the ground and using special equipment to create extremely close-up photos.

I've flown in helicopters and small airplanes to get views of wild animals from above. This is hard for me because I get sick in small planes. Sometimes I have to switch between being sick in a bag and taking pictures, over and over again. It's not pleasant, but that doesn't stop me from trying to get the shot!

Do not disturb

As a wildlife photographer, I do my best not to disturb my subjects. I always try to make sure that the animals are relaxed and comfortable with my presence. It respects the animals, and it's also the best way to get special pictures. When animals feel safe, they act naturally and forget that I am even there.

Getting an animal to trust me can take a long time—sometimes days or weeks. I keep my distance at first and then move closer and closer over time. I always move slowly and quietly. Sometimes, I avoid even making eye contact. Gradually, the animals learn that they can trust me. They come to know that I won't hurt them.

Some animals get so comfortable with me that I become part of their habitat. These meerkats are using me to block the wind. It made a great shot for the photographer that I was with, though.

Being respectful of animals also helps keep me safe. Many animals feel threatened when people get too close. Some, such as bears and big cats, can be deadly when they defend themselves. I use a long lens to photograph these animals. I can stand far away and still get close-up photos.

I took this photo using a long lens. It may seem as though I was very close to this grizzly bear and her cubs, but I was actually about 50 yards (46 meters) away. Sometimes bears get curious and come too close to me, though. I try to scare them off with a loud noise first, but I always carry bear spray in case that doesn't work. But in fifteen years of photographing bears, I've never had to use bear spray.

Mothers and babies

Ever since I was a small child, I have loved baby animals. They are my favorite subjects to photograph, but animal mothers make it challenging. They can be extra alert and protective.

For some of my best mother-and-baby shots, it took me weeks to gain the mother's trust and get close enough to take pictures. Once I got close, I spent months photographing the animal families. I spent five months on safari with a jackal family, two months at a tiger den, and eighteen months with five different cheetah families. Every day, I was with an animal family from sunrise to sunset, just quietly watching and taking pictures.

Seeing baby animals grow up is my greatest joy. It's so much fun to watch them change from tiny, helpless beings into big, strong adults. And I get to see them discover new things, like leaving their den and seeing the outside world for the first time or making their first kill.

I followed this cheetah mother when she was pregnant. Since she was already used to me, I was able to photograph her tiny, newborn cubs when they were only four days old. Seeing baby animals this young in the wild is very rare and special. I felt so honored that this cheetah mother trusted me to be there.

Mothers are very good at hiding their newborn babies, so sometimes the greatest challenge is finding them. For my tiger-cub project, it took ten days just to find the den. The mother had given birth inside a cave, where the cubs were safely stashed away from predators and kept cool in the monsoon heat.

Rescues and orphans

I have photographed hundreds of wild animals, but I have only touched a few. Wildlife photographers generally do not touch animals. There are a few reasons why. Most wild animals don't like human contact. It causes them great stress. When some animals are spooked, they can hurt themselves or others in their panic. Other animals may attack people when they feel threatened.

Another danger of interacting with wild animals is making them too comfortable around people. When animals no longer fear people, they may approach cars, camps, homes, or towns, where they may be hurt or killed.

There are times when humans and wild animals do need to interact, though. People sometimes need to touch injured animals to help them and treat their wounds. When I was working in Australia, I photographed quite a few koalas that were hit by cars. Wildlife rehabilitators cared for the koalas until they were well enough to be released to the wild.

Animals who live where people live face unique challenges, like this rescued egret and koala. They were hit by cars. If you see an animal that is hurt or in distress, call your local wildlife rescue center.

Orphaned or abandoned baby animals also need to be touched to survive. In Borneo, I photographed orphaned orangutans who rely on people to take the place of their mothers. The caretakers groom and play with the babies and carry them on their backs the same way an orangutan mother would. It takes seven years to teach an orphaned orangutan all the skills it will need to survive in the wild. When an orphan is ready to return to the wild, caretakers gently break the human-animal bond over time.

When I was photographing at an Orangutan Foundation International's orphanage, I was lucky enough to hold one of the babies. I had to be very careful. I wore a mask and gloves. Orangutans can easily catch illnesses from humans, and even a little cold can be deadly for them.

Learning from locals

This is me with Kambango, a tracker I worked with in Botswana.

I feel lucky to have had the chance to work with amazing people from different cultures all over the world. Although I often work alone, sometimes it takes a team effort to photograph hard-to-find species. I work with local guides and trackers, who are experts at locating sneaky animals. They also know animal behaviors and habits, so they can tell me where and when to be on the lookout.

To photograph a leopard mother and cubs in Botswana, I worked very closely with a tracker named Kambango. He had known the leopard mother for eight years, so he knew all her favorite places. Kambango could find her by looking for her tracks on the ground. It's amazing what he knew just by looking at a paw print. He could tell if the leopard was male or female, how old it was, and sometimes even what it was doing!

Without Kambango's help, I could never have captured this adorable photo of a leopard cleaning her tiny cub.

I also work with locals who are active in conservation. In Vietnam, I worked with a man named Thai who has dedicated his life to saving pangolins. Thai cares for pangolins that have been rescued from poachers. He also spends time explaining to local communities why pangolins are in danger of disappearing. He encourages people not to hunt them.

This is Thai with a pangolin he rescued.

I loved sharing my photos of the zebras with Samburu villagers.

In Kenya, I partnered with Samburu women who share their well water with endangered Grévy's zebras. Many Samburu villagers don't allow wildlife to drink at their wells, but these women let the zebras drink in peace. It is very dry where they live, and the zebras would die of thirst without this water.

Working with scientists

It's inspiring to meet people all over the world who love animals as much as I do. Throughout my career, I have been lucky to partner with scientists who have spent their lives studying wildlife and ecosystems.

Scientists are always learning new information about wild animals. Sometimes they even discover new species. Their research can show us how to help save animals and their habitats.

Many scientists work directly with wildlife to measure, weigh, examine, and treat animals. Sometimes, when they need an extra hand, I get to join in. Working with scientists has allowed me to experience things that wouldn't be possible in the wild, such as getting a close-up view of a polar bear's teeth or touching a sea otter's incredibly soft fur.

While working with a team of polar bear researchers, I got to hold a cub to keep it warm. The cub had been medicated and slept peacefully in my arms. This is an experience I will remember forever!

I've spent a lot of time with cheetahs in the wild, but I never had the chance to listen to one's heart before meeting Dr. Laurie Marker. She invited me to hear this cheetah's heartbeat while she gave it a health exam. I got to feel its heartbeat, too!

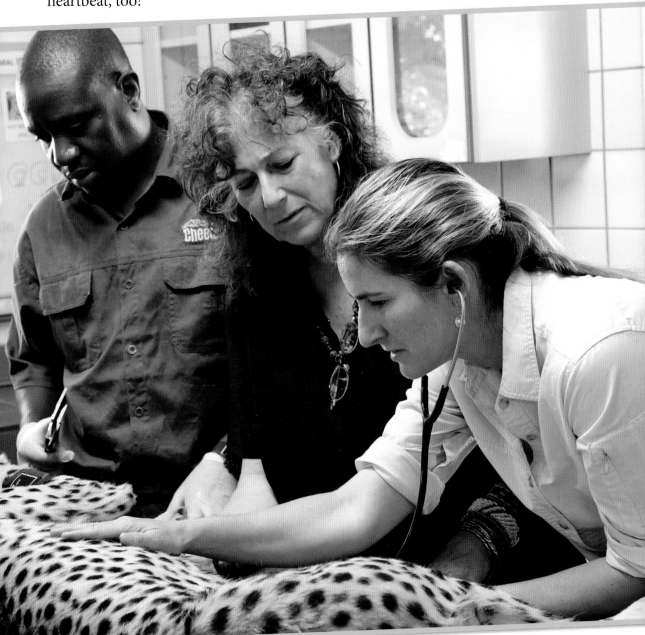

I got to hear for myself how fast a cheetah's heart beats. Even when resting, its heart beats at a similar rate to that of a person jogging.

Giving back to animals

This is one of the most playful moments I have ever captured. Cheetah cubs can be very feisty and love to pounce on things—especially their mom's head!

Being a wildlife photographer will not make me rich, and I am okay with that. I do what I do because I love animals. They have given me so much joy that I feel a huge responsibility to give back to them.

Many of the species I have photographed are endangered. They are at risk of becoming extinct because of climate change, habitat loss, poaching, and other problems caused by people. So I don't just collect pretty pictures of these animals. I use my photos and my voice to raise money and awareness for conservation.

Cheetahs were one of my first dream subjects. I saved money for years to make that dream photo shoot a reality. It was expensive to buy equipment, travel, and live in faraway places for months at a time. But in the end, it was worth it!

Cheetahs are endangered due to habitat loss, and I wanted to do something to help them. So I used my photos to publish a book with a cheetah expert and sold it to raise money for the Cheetah Conservation Fund. I also give talks about the Fund's work to teach people what they can do to help save cheetahs.

Sloths are threatened in many areas of Central and South America. I spent four weeks photographing injured and orphaned sloths at a rescue center in Costa Rica. I fell in love with these sweet, slow-moving animals, so I partnered with the Sloth Conservation Foundation to help raise money to save them. The group sells books and calendars that feature my sloth photos.

Like cheetahs, lions are disappearing fast, mostly due to hunting and habitat loss. I use my lion photos to help raise awareness for the Wildlife Conservation Network. This group works hard to save lions across Africa.

I love this photo because it gives us a glimpse into a sloth's upside-down life.

This is one of my favorite—and best-selling—photos. It shows a lion dad meeting his cub for the first time. I followed the family and waited for weeks before capturing this very special moment.

Ask Suzi

I get asked a lot of questions about what it's like to be a wildlife photographer. These are some of the questions I get asked most often.

What is the best part of your job?

When I'm in the field photographing wildlife, every day is different. Some days, my animal subjects do nothing exciting and sleep all day. On other days, they never stop—hunting, playing, avoiding predators, and so on.

What is the hardest part of your job?

Waiting! Some people think being a wildlife photographer means nonstop action, but animals aren't always doing exciting things. In fact, most of my time is spent waiting for something to happen. Waiting quietly is really hard work!

How do I become a wildlife photographer?

Practice taking pictures, learn as much as you can about animals, and be ready to work hard. Wildlife photography won't make you rich, but you will have adventure, a life outdoors, time with animals, and a job that you love.

Sometimes the hardest part of my job is staying awake! While I was lying on the forest floor watching a sloth in the tree above, I accidentally fell asleep. Oops! Luckily, the sloth researcher with me stayed wide awake.

Have people treated you differently as a wildlife photographer because you're a woman?

Unfortunately, yes—especially when I was starting out. Some people think that women are not tough or strong enough to do this job. Wildlife photographers are almost all men, but there is no reason why women can't do this job, too! It's one of the reasons I started Girls Who Click. I wanted to help other girls live their dream of becoming wildlife photographers. You can learn more at www.girlswhoclick.org.

If my family doesn't travel, can I still do wildlife photography?

Absolutely! You can take photos of wildlife in your own community. You may not have lions and elephants living in your neighborhood, but even the most urban environments have parks where small animals, such as insects and birds, live. You might be surprised at the natural life you find once you start looking. You can also photograph the plants and landscapes in your area.

If I don't have a camera, how can I take pictures?

You don't need a fancy camera; if you have access to a device that takes pictures, such as a smartphone or tablet, you can photograph the world around you. Even without a device, you can practice patience, observe animal behavior, go camping or hiking, and spend as much time as you can learning about animals around the world.

What is your most incredible wildlife experience so far?

Swimming with humpback whales. These gentle giants made me feel so small! But there are still so many animals that I want to photograph— such as bonobos, harp seals, emperor penguins. I have lots of adventures waiting for me!

This book is dedicated to Owen and Amanda, who helped me begin my journey. I will forever be grateful for your kindness, guidance, and friendship.

Owlkids Books acknowledges the financial support of the Canada Council for the Arts, the Ontario Arts Council, the Government of Canada through the Canada Book Fund (CBF) and the Government of Ontario through the Ontario Creates Book Initiative for our publishing activities.

Published in Canada by
Owlkids Books Inc.
1 Eglinton Avenue East
Toronto, ON M4P 3A1

Published in the United States by
Owlkids Books Inc.
1700 Fourth Street
Berkeley, CA 94710

J-B
ESZTERHAS
479-6549

Library of Congress Control Number: 2019956481

Library and Archives Canada Cataloguing in Publication

Title: My wild life: adventures of a wildlife photographer / by Suzi Eszterhas.
Names: Eszterhas, Suzi, author, photographer.
Identifiers: Canadiana 20200161105 | ISBN 9781771474078 (hardcover)
Subjects: LCSH: Eszterhas, Suzi—Juvenile literature. | LCSH: Wildlife photographers—Biography—Juvenile literature. | LCSH: Wildlife photography—Juvenile literature. | LCSH: Human-animal relationships—Juvenile literature.
Classification: LCC TR140 .E89 2020 | DDC j770.92—dc23

Edited by Niki Walker

Designed by Danielle Arbour

Photo credits: Front cover: Jak Wonderly; pages 1, 2: Arlene Davis; 5: Jak Wonderly; 6: Jak Wonderly (top); 8: Graham Racher (upper); 8: Jak Wonderly (lower); 11: Rebecca Cliffe (middle); 12: Jak Wonderly (upper); 16: Jak Wonderly (both); 18: Jak Wonderly; 19: Jak Wonderly (upper); 22: Jak Wonderly (upper); 27: Susan Janin; 30: Rebecca Cliffe (left); 31: Michelle Stern (upper).

ONTARIO ARTS COUNCIL
CONSEIL DES ARTS DE L'ONTARIO
an Ontario government agency
un organisme du gouvernement de l'Ontario

 Canada Council for the Arts   Conseil des Arts du Canada

Canadä

Manufactured in Guangdong Province, Dongguan City, China, in April 2020, by Toppan Leefung Packaging & Printing (Dongguan) Co., Ltd.   Job # BAYDC75

A   B   C   D   E   F

 Publisher of Chirp, Chickadee and OWL
www.owlkidsbooks.com | Owlkids Books is a division of  bayard canada